AF302539

INFLATION-CONSCIOUS INVESTMENTS

Avoid the most common investment pitfalls

Written by Guillaume Steffens
Translated by Emma Hanna

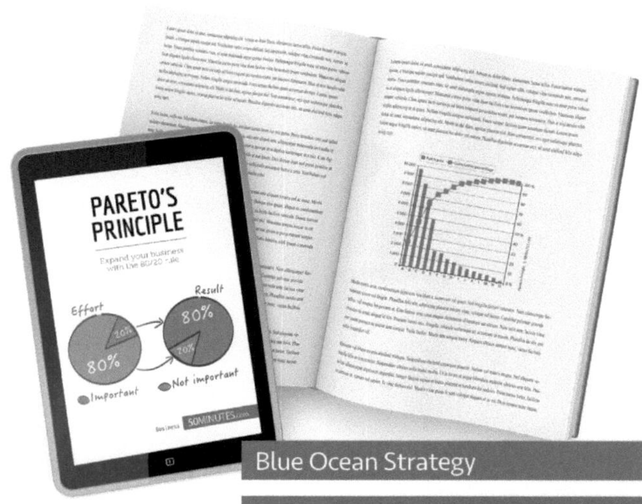

50MINUTES.com

PROPEL
YOUR BUSINESS FORWARD!

PARETO'S PRINCIPLE
Expand your business
with the 80/20 rule

Effort
20%
80%
Important

Result
80%
20%
Not important

Business   50MINUTES.com

Blue Ocean Strategy

Pareto's Principle

Managing Stress at Work

Game Theory

www.50minutes.com

INFLATION-CONSCIOUS INVESTMENTS

- **Problem:** what do overall and long-term price increases mean and how can you figure out the total amount that they represent? What specific consequences does inflation have on the purchasing power and decision-making capacities of households and businesses? How can you take this limiting variable into account when investing?
- **Uses:** national and international statistical institutes calculate inflation rates in order to determine the rates of overall and specific price increases within a certain period. Given that price and salary increases do not remain proportional during periods of inflation, it may be necessary to monitor their fluctuations in order to:
  - limit their negative effects and try to balance the relationships between the major macroeconomic indicators of inflation, unemployment and GDP;

- estimate the real gains that could be generated by current investments over the short, medium (10-20 years) and long term (50 years or more);
- relativise a country's economic development by differentiating the growth due to price increases from the growth due to an increase in production volume.

- **Key words:**
  - <u>Constant price</u>: corresponding price during the reference year.
  - <u>Consumer basket</u>: the consumer basket is one method of measuring inflation and the cost of living. It is made up of a set of consumer products which are used to measure how prices vary over time.
  - <u>Current price</u>: corresponding price during the period in question.
  - <u>Nominal value</u>: an amount which does not take the effects of inflation into account (the first total which is calculated).
  - <u>Purchasing power</u>: the ability to buy a certain quantity of goods in exchange for a certain quantity of money.
  - <u>Real value</u>: an amount which takes the effects of inflation into account.

Given that inflation, like unemployment and GDP, is one of the primary concerns of national and international financial institutions, it is essential to have a good understanding of it in order to effectively shield yourself from the effects of factors associated with it. All investors should stay well-informed about any financial trends or incidents which could affect their portfolio.

Basic concepts

- **Inflation:** sustained overall price increases. The lower a country's overall price level, the more its currency will be worth. If this overall price level increases, it is known as inflation, and this reduces the country's purchasing power. In other words, the quantity of goods which can be purchased with a fixed sum of money in that currency will be reduced.
- **Deflation:** an overall drop in prices, which is the inverse of inflation.
- **Disinflation:** a drop in the rate of inflation, meaning that prices will continue to rise but more slowly.
- **Hyperinflation:** a period of extreme

inflation.

Within the Eurozone, the European Central Bank is in charge of combatting inflation. Its goal is to keep the rate of inflation close to but no higher than 2%.

As such, investors must always bear in mind the fact that currencies tend to lose value as a result of inflation. The current value of one pound will almost certainly have changed by tomorrow. This means that expecting the final value of your pension to correspond to current currency values can lead to disappointment. Here is a more concrete example: a 165 m^2 house might be worth £150 000 today, but in 40 years, that sum may only be enough to buy a 45 m^2 flat. Fortunately, we can use mathematical formulae to convert sums of money according to predicted levels of inflation. This is what we will be explaining in this book.

DID YOU KNOW?

In order to compete in the global economy, certain countries try to keep their prices low. In order to do so, they can devalue their currency, which makes it more attractive to their trading partners. More rarely, governments may trigger deflation, meaning an internal price drop. This is what Pierre Laval's government did in France in 1935, by drastically reducing public spending to reduce the public's purchasing power, causing both demand and prices to fall.

THEORY

THE INEVITABILITY OF INFLATION

Most countries are affected by inflation, although long or short periods of deflation can also occur. The graph below provides an overview of these fluctuations over the past two decades, using prices in 2005 as a reference point for each country or region. We can see that these prices are constantly increasing.

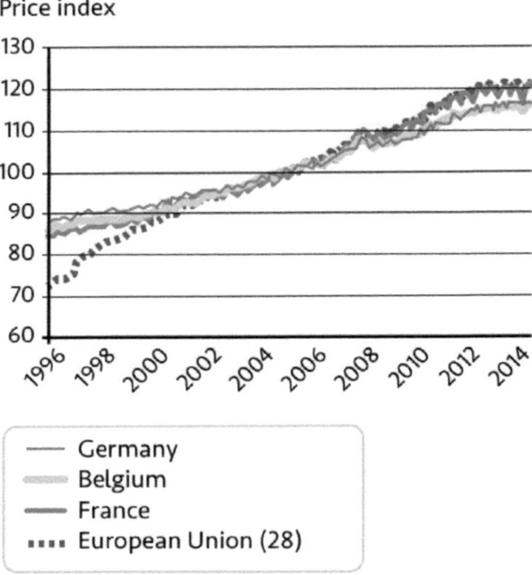

This graph charts inflation on a monthly basis according to a "household shopping basket". The 2005 "basket" acts as a reference point (inflation in 2005 = 100). By 2015, prices had increased by 20% compared to 2005 in the European Union (inflation in 2015 = 120).

© 50MINUTES.com

What causes it?

Inflation can be caused by several different factors: money supply, demand, costs, financial predictions or changing consumer habits.

- **Money supply:** Irving Fisher (American economist, 1867-1947) claimed that increases in monetary supplies cause inflation and that spending totals should be kept equal to sales totals in order to prevent it. The spending total can be defined by the total money supply in circulation (M) multiplied by the velocity of the money (V), meaning the frequency with which a unit of money changes hands. Meanwhile, the sales total is equal to the price level (P) multiplied by transaction volume (T). This can be represented by the mathematical formula $M*V = P*T$. According to monetarists, the velocity of the money (V) and the transaction volume (T) will remain constant in the short term. Consequently, if the total money supply in circulation (M) increases, the price level (P) will also increase. According to Milton Friedman (American economist, 1912-2006), all inflation can be traced back to causes related to the money supply.
- **Demand:** according to John Maynard Keynes (British economist, 1883-1946), inflation is not a purely monetary phenomenon, and can also be caused when demand outstrips supply. In the classic model of supply and demand, an in-

crease in demand will lead to a corresponding rise in prices.

THE CLASSIC MODEL OF SUPPLY AND DEMAND

In his book *Principles of Economics*, which was first published in 1890, Alfred Marshall introduced the idea of supply and demand curves, which appear in many economic handbooks (with quantity along the horizontal axis, price on the vertical axis, a decreasing demand curve and an increasing supply curve).

This model has evolved and been adapted by many different economists over the years. The British economist Adam Smith (1723-1790) examined the relationship between supply and demand in his book *An Inquiry into the Nature and Causes of the Wealth of Nations* (1776); later, Antoine-Augustin Cournot (French mathematician, 1801-1877) considered the notions of duopoly, monopoly and competition in his book *Researches on the Mathematical Principles of the Theory of Wealth* (1838).

- **Costs:** while production costs are increasing, companies will be tempted to compensate by raising the prices of the goods or services they offer. Notable examples of periods when this phenomenon could be observed include the petrol crises of 1973 and 1979, as oil was one of the critical factors which determined production costs. Nowadays, the other factors which contribute to rising costs, in addition to oil, include rising salaries and tax hikes. This results in rising prices and, by extension, inflation. When the price of imported products increases, this is known as "imported inflation".

- **Financial predictions:** when economists predict price increases, their attempts to alleviate this problem will actually cause a certain degree of inflation. In practice, households will end up requesting higher salaries (which drives up costs and, by extension, inflation) and businesses will raise their prices in order to keep profits steady, thus causing inflation to spiral.

- **Changing consumer habits:** if consumer habits change suddenly, demand will increase in certain sectors to the detriment of others. This can have serious consequences, such as increased unemployment and inflation.

Inflation and unemployment

William Phillips (New Zealand economist, 1914-1975) empirically demonstrated the negative correlation between the unemployment rate and the rate of inflation, and used a mathematical curve (which was named after him) to visualise this relationship.

- A drop in the unemployment rate will cause some short-term inflation. In practice, this means that it will be more difficult for businesses to find staff to hire and that employees will be able to take advantage of this by asking for higher salaries, which will in turn increase costs.
- The Non Accelerating Inflation Rate of Unemployment (NAIRU) is the level of unemployment at which inflation will be stable. This level varies by country and is taken into account when predicting inflation.
- According to monetarist theory, the relationship between unemployment and inflation will become unstable in the long term. When employees observe that prices have increased,

they will request raises, which will lead to further price increases, causing inflation to spiral. Economic recovery policies (which aim to reduce unemployment) also contribute to inflation, and even if the unemployment rate can be brought back down to its original level, the rate of inflation will continue to increase.

The consequences of inflation

Inflation causes increased costs, which have an impact on both households and businesses but also offer certain advantages.

Advantages and disadvantages

Disadvantages
• **Decreased purchasing power**, because most products will become more expensive. Consumers will therefore be unable to continue buying as much on the same salary.
• **Reduced competition** due to the increase in the price of domestic products compared to the prices of products produced globally. However, according to the theory of purchasing power parity, when the rate of inflation increases, the exchange rate decreases proportionally. As the currency depreciates, it rebalances the situation.
• **"Shoe leather costs"** or the time and effort associated with keeping the majority of your money in the bank, as is recommended during times of high inflation due to the corresponding rise in interest rates. Historically, this referred to the fact that going to the bank to withdraw money more often led to shoes being worn out more quickly.

Disadvantages

- **Increased "menu costs":** companies will have to update their catalogues, menus or advertisements more often to reflect changing prices.

- **General uncertainty** which makes investors and entrepreneurs more hesitant during periods of high inflation.

- **Significantly higher capital gains taxes,** which are calculated by subtracting the purchase value from the resale value in periods of high inflation.

- **The money illusion,** which makes it difficult to calculate the consequences of inflation, as shown by Shafir, Diamond and Tversky. The money illusion leads individuals to base their decisions on nominal values (which do not take inflation into account) rather than real values (which take inflation into account).

- **Saving erosion,** as money which is placed in a savings account loses value according to the rate of inflation.

<table>
<tr><th>Advantages</th></tr>
<tr><td>

- **Increased value of imported products,** which will become less expensive in comparison to domestic products as the latter increase in price. However, exchange rates will fluctuate.

- **Considerable staff increases,** because a certain degree of inflation reduces real salaries and makes it possible for businesses to hire more staff (thus reducing unemployment).

- **Debt erosion,** because unlike savers, borrowers will be able to pay back their loans more easily.

</td></tr>
</table>

WAGE INDEXATION

Inflation causes a decrease in households' purchasing power, and certain countries attempt to offset this through wage indexation, meaning that salaries are increased proportional to inflation. Although this system has been criticised, it is used in various countries, including Belgium, Luxembourg, Cyprus, Malta and Spain (through collective labour agreements).

DEFLATION

As a reminder, deflation is the opposite of in-flation, and can be defined as a relatively long period of time (more than a quarter) when the overall price level falls. This trend, which may seem beneficial for consumers, can actually cause problems for the global economy.

When economic agents realise that prices are falling, they will delay making purchases (as they will believe that prices will be even lower tomorrow) and therefore slow down economic growth. If this situation continues, companies will adjust their production according to demand and may be forced to lay off some of their staff. This massive increase in unemployment will also have negative consequences on global demand, as households will have less disposable income, which will lead to a further drop in prices, cau-sing deflation to spiral.

Unlike inflation, deflation puts lenders at an advantage and borrowers at a disadvantage.

While a currency's value is increasing, individuals benefit from receiving money tomorrow instead of today, as their purchasing power will increase. Following this logic, it becomes more difficult for households to pay back their debts while their salaries are in freefall.

PRACTICAL APPLICATION

HOW TO REACT TO THESE SITUATIONS

Before making any investment decisions, it is essential to have a good understanding of the mechanisms related to inflation. Any discerning investor should follow these principles:

- Never act as though tomorrow's money is already in your pocket.
- When making an investment or opening a pension fund, estimate the rate of inflation and calculate the current value of the capital which will be accumulated.
- Borrow money during periods of inflation instead of lending: invest in stock, real estate (as rent is usually indexed according to infla-tion) or raw materials (which have high yields but which are not necessarily available to the general public). You should also consider in-vesting in less risky commodities such as gold

or silver.

- In periods of deflation, buy bonds at a fixed rate or invest in fixed term accounts, because getting into debt or buying stock is inadvisable when there is a chance that deflation could spiral and cause growth to falter.

HOW TO SPOT PRICE FLUCTUATIONS

In the European Union, the system used to calculate inflation is known as the Harmonised Index of Consumer Prices (HICP), and allows international comparisons to be drawn. This index is calculated using a "consumer basket" comprising the goods consumed within a country or region and is weighted according to the population's real spending habits. It includes food, durable goods (cars, computers, etc.) and services (insurance, rent, etc.). Its contents change over time to match consumer trends (for example, almond milk was added to the British index in 2017, and the fee for stopping a cheque was removed).

The table below illustrates how national and international statistical institutes use this imaginary shopping basket to calculate inflation.

Consumer basket contents	Price (reference year)	
	Unit price	Total price
100 apples	£0.30	£30
50x400g brown bread	£1.30	£65
10 haircuts	£15	£150
2 shirts	£20	£40
Total cost		£285
Price index		100
Rate of inflation		

Consumer basket contents	Price (one year later) Year 2	
	Unit price	Total price
100 apples	£0.25	£25
50x400g brown bread	£1.40	£70
10 haircuts	£16	£160
2 shirts	£22	£44
Total cost		£299
Price index	299/285 *100	104.91
Rate of inflation		4.91%

Consumer basket contents	Price (two years later) Year 3	
	Unit price	Total price
100 apples	£0.35	£35
50x400g brown bread	£1.40	£70
10 haircuts	£17	£170
2 shirts	£25	£50
Total cost		£325
Price index	325/285 *100	114.035
Rate of inflation	(325/299) *(100)-100	**8.70%**

1. First, the relevant statistical institute determines which products should be included in the reference basket, as well as their prices and quantities.
2. Next, the prices of these items are added together to find the total cost of the basket, which is used as a reference for the rest of the calculations. By applying the same principle

the following year, it is possible to compare the basket from the following year with the reference year.

3. The total cost of the basket (from the year of your choice) is divided by the total cost of the basket from the reference year to find the price index. For year 2 in the example provided, the calculation would be 299/285*100 = 104.91. This index shows that prices are 4.91% higher than in the reference year.

4. The rate of inflation corresponds to the variation in the basket prices from year to year. There are two possible methods of calculating the rate of inflation for year 3:

   ◦ dividing the cost of the basket from year 3 by the cost of the basket from year 2, then multiplying the result by 100, or 325/299*(100)-100 = 8.70%;
   ◦ or subtracting the cost of the basket from year 2 from the cost of the basket from year 3, then dividing the result by the price index from year 2 and multiplying it by 100, or (114.035-104.91)/104.91*100 = 8.70%.

Both of these methods will give you the same result: in year 3, prices are 14.04% higher than they were in the reference year, and 8.7% higher than in year 2.

You should note that in this example, not all of the goods went up in price, and some even became cheaper – specifically, apples became cheaper between the reference year and year 2. This means that the rate of inflation measures the average price increase.

DID YOU KNOW?

The organisations which calculate these indexes are sworn to statistical secrecy. Although their results are made public, the data for each product is not made public. For example, it is not possible to find out the prices set by a specific supermarket for a particular product.

CASE STUDIES

We will now take a detailed look at the consequences for borrowers and lenders, starting with some simple cases.

Simple case: a one-off loan (borrower's perspective)

In this first case we will consider an example involving a person who wants to buy a house. They go to their bank with the aim of borrowing the £100 000 they need. Their bank offers them an annual interest rate of 4% over 20 years. By the end of this period of time, the borrower will have had to pay back £144 532.50. However, this does not take the rate of inflation into account.

Each year, the real value of the original £144 532.50 will fall due to the rate of inflation, which will be assumed to be 2% in this example. The table below shows how the overall value of the repayments will vary from year to year when this rate of inflation is taken into account.

N	£144 532.50
N+1	£144 532.50/1.02 = £141 698.53
N+2	£141 698.53/1.02 = £138 920.13
N+3	£138 920.13/1.02 = £136 196.20
N+4	...
N+5	£97 266.23

Every year, the real value of the repayments will diminish by 2% in comparison to the previous year. We know what the future value (S_n) is, but we do not know the present value (S_0), meaning the equivalent value of this sum at the end of the 20 years in today's money. The present value rises by a constant yearly rate (t), which can be simplified to that rate raised to the power of the number of years (n). By multiplying this figure by the present value, the final value can be obtained: ($S_n = S_0*(1 + t)^n$).

This formula can be rearranged to calculate the present value:

$$Sum\ invested * \frac{1}{(1 + estimated\ rate\ of\ inflation)^{number\ of\ years}}$$

In this example, we will get this result:

$$£144\ 532.50 * \frac{1}{(1 + 0.02)^{20}} = £97\ 266.23$$

This means that inflation benefits borrowers. As the years go by, their monthly repayments will gradually become a smaller proportion of their monthly budget because their purchasing power is decreasing consistently.

Simple case: one-off savings

In this example we will be considering a saver who deposits £1000 into a fixed-term account for five years at a nominal yearly interest rate of 5%. In the first year, the saver will receive £1000*5/100 = £50 in interest. By leaving this interest in the account, it will also generate interest in the following years (compound interest). In the second year, the saver will receive £1050*5/100 = £52.5 in interest, and so on. The table below summarises how interest is generated across all five years:

N	£1000
N+1	£1000 + £1000 * (5/100) = £1050
N+2	£1050 + £1050 * (5/100) = £1102.50
N+3	£1157.63
N+4	£1215.51
N+5	£1276.28

This table can be summarised using the following formula:

$$(1 + interest\ rate)^{number\ of\ time\ periods}$$

In this specific example, this gives us:

$$(1 + 0.05)^5 * £1000 = £1276.28$$

It is important to take inflation into account

when considering this sum of money, which the saver will receive in five years. The table below shows how the overall value of the final amount to be repaid will vary over the years, taking an estimated yearly rate of inflation of 2% into account.

N	£1276.28
N+1	£1276.28/1.02 = £1251.26
N+2	£1251.26/1.02 = £1226.72
N+3	£1226.72/1.02 = £1202.67
N+4	£1202.67/1.02 = £1179.09
N+5	£1179.09/1.02 = £1155.97

If a yearly rate of inflation of 2% is taken into account, the £1276.28 will be worth no more than £1155.97 after five years. The higher the rate of inflation, the more the savings account's purchasing power will decrease. The formula above can be reused in order to calculate how much this sum will be worth in year 5 when the rate of inflation is taken into account:

$$£1276.28 * \frac{1}{(1 + 0.02)^5} = £1155.97$$

Taking inflation into account, the real sum which the saver (the borrower) will receive at the end of the five years will be lower. Conversely, the bank (the lender) has been able to use a sum of money which is worth more in year N than when it has to pay the saver in the year N + 5.

Periodic payments (annuities)

We will now consider an example in which a saver wishes to set up a pension fund and makes a yearly deposit of £1000 for 15 years at a 4% interest rate. In year N, the saver places £1000 in the account, which generates £1000*4/100 = £40 in interest in year N + 1. This £40 in interest is left in the account in the year N + 1, and another £1000 is added to the account, creating a total of £2040 and generating £2040*4/100 = £81.60 in interest for year N + 2, and so on.

This mathematical process can be summarised by the formula below, which allows the total obtained in year 15 to be calculated:

$$\textit{Periodically deposited sum} * \frac{(1 + \textit{interest rate})^{\text{number of time periods}} - 1}{\textit{interest rate}}$$

In this example, this works out as:

$$£1000 * \frac{(1 + 0.04)^{15} - 1}{0.04} = £20\ 023.59$$

This total represents the sum that the saver will receive in 15 years. When the bank gives the saver this figure, they will think of it in terms of the current economy. However, by taking inflation into account it becomes clear that this amount will not be worth as much in 15 years as it is to-day. As such, the current value of this sum needs to be calculated. We can use the same formula we used in the simple case study to calculate the current value of the final total: £20 023.59*1/(1+0.02)^{15} = £14 877.82.

In the absence of interest but taking a 2% rate

of inflation into account, this annuity has a redemption price which can be calculated as follows: £1000*1 − (1+0.02)$^{-15}$ = £12 849.26. In other words, by taking a 2% rate of inflation into account, the sum of the payments of £1000 across all 15 years – meaning £15 000 in total – is actually equivalent to a purchasing power of £12 849.26 in the current economy. The interest rate that the bank offers the saver must be greater than the rate of inflation for this to represent a positive yield in real terms. In this example, the rate of inflation is 2%, so the total final savings must be greater than 1000*(1+0.02)15 - 1/0.02 = £17 293.41 to represent an overall profit.

The following formula is used to convert the nominal interest rate into a real interest rate:

$$(1 + \textit{nominal interest rate}) =$$
$$(1 + \textit{real interest rate}) * (1 + \textit{rate of inflation})$$

The real interest rate can only be estimated, because it is obviously impossible to predict what the exact rate of inflation will be over the following years. In this example, the estimated rate is 1.04/1.02 – 1*100 = 1.96%, because 1.04 = 1.0196*1.02. This prediction plays a crucial role, even though it is impossible to accurately predict what the real rate of inflation will be ahead of time.

General simulation

It is extremely important to understand the ideas which we have addressed thus far in order to make smart investments. Consider the following situations a saver could face:

	Nominal yield rate	Rate of inflation
Situation 1	5%	6%
Situation 2	3%	2%
Situation 3	3%	-2%

- In situation 1, the rate of inflation is higher than the nominal yield rate, which means that the yield is completely negated by inflation. Unsurprisingly, the real yield is negative:

1.05/1.06 – 1*100 = -0.94%.

- In situation 2, the nominal yield rate is greater than the rate of inflation, which is more advantageous for the saver than the first scenario. The real yield rate is 1.03/1.02 – 1*100 = 0.98%.
- In situation 3, the economy is experiencing deflation, and prices are falling instead of rising, which is advantageous for the saver. The real yield rate is the most favourable of all three situations: 1.03/0.98 – 1*100 = 5.10%.

These situations provide an illustration of the phenomenon of money illusion that was explained previously. At first glance, the first situation might seem the most beneficial, since it offers the highest nominal yield rate, but it is actually the least profitable because of the critical role played by inflation. Take it into account before you make any investment decisions!

You should also bear in mind that interest rates are partially determined by inflation. During periods of high inflation, central banks tend to raise policy interest rates (the rates used as a reference for both deposits and credit). They also encourage economic agents to invest their money and dissuade them from borrowing to make investments. This reduces demand and the inflation caused by excess demand. The opposite phenomenon will occur when inflation is low, which means that it will be difficult to secure high interest rates when inflation is low, and vice versa.

IMPACT

LIMITATIONS AND CRITICISMS

- **The reliability of available consumer basket statistics (contents and total cost).** The method used to measure inflation is the aspect of this model which is most frequently criticised. The French consumer association UFC Que Choisir has created its own price index. It takes a smaller number of products and services into consideration, but the index is higher than the one calculated by INSEE, the French institute for statistics, and therefore implies that inflation is higher than the rate indicated by the official index. The lack of transparency regarding the exact products which are included in the index (because some countries reveal more about which products are included than others) is understandable, but it makes it impossible for consumers to determine whether or not the index is truly reliable. The index aims to reflect household spending as accurately as possible and therefore also includes certain goods and services which are used less frequently, and which some individuals may never actually use (e.g. tanning beds).

- **The fierce battle against inflation.** The European Central Bank's purpose is to keep inflation steady at a level which is close to but does not exceed 2% within the European Union. However, certain authors (Akerlof, Dickens and Perry) claim that in a crisis, rising inflation (beyond 2%) can be beneficial. In practice, when companies struggle to hold on to their staff because of economic slowdown, they have to choose between reducing their employees' wages and laying some of them off. Since nominal salary cuts often create significant employee dissatisfaction, raising the rate of inflation can produce the same effect and therefore prevent mass layoffs while also forestalling the dissatisfaction that would have been caused by reducing nominal wages (since real salaries will experience a drop anyway). Inflation can also be used to revitalise the economy. In practice, it encourages economic agents to spend money, because they will be able to use the same sum of money to buy more today than they will be able to buy tomorrow. Finally, low inflation is beneficial to annuitants, but detrimental to entrepreneurs, and it is advantageous for lenders but makes it more difficult for borrowers to pay back their loans.

EXTENSIONS AND RELATED CONCEPTS

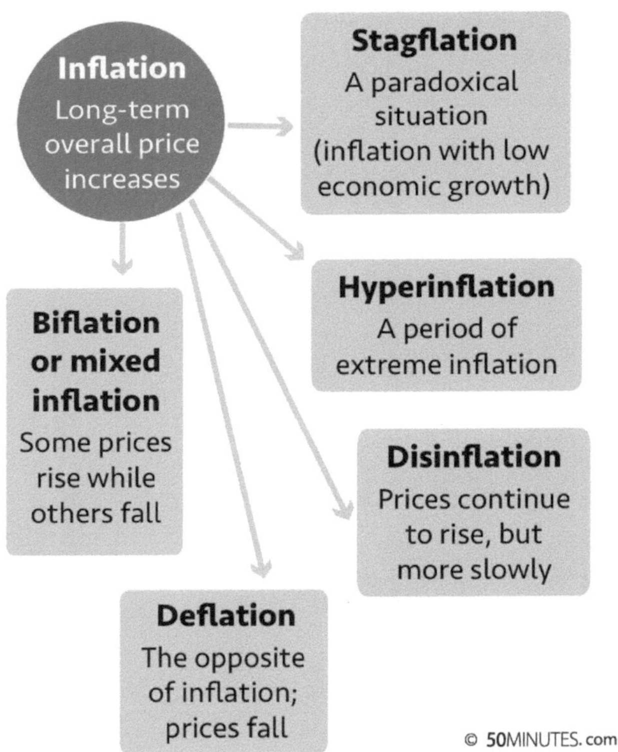

- **Hyperinflation:** this refers to a period of extreme inflation. Philip Cagan (American economist, 1927-2012) defined it as a situation in which prices are rising by 50% or more each month. In this specific case, people will prefer to use a different, more stable currency.

- **Stagflation:** this word is a contraction of the terms "economic stagnation" and "inflation", and denotes a situation in which there is low economic growth despite inflation. This paradoxical situation can be explained by inflation being caused by the money supply or costs, and not demand. For example, the oil crisis in 1973 caused a period of stagflation.
- **Disinflation:** should not be confused with deflation. Disinflation refers to a situation in which prices continue to rise, but at a slower rate than normal inflation.
- **Biflation or mixed inflation:** these two terms refer to the same concept: a situation in which certain prices are rising while others are falling simultaneously. For example, the price of food could be rising while real estate prices are in freefall. In a recession or during times of low economic activity, households will continue to buy food but will no longer invest in household goods or cars, for example. This is another blow to the theory which visualises inflation

using a consumer basket that contains durable goods, given that an overall price increase and inflation are not mutually inclusive situations. As we have already seen, it is possible for certain prices to decrease during a period of inflation.

DID YOU KNOW?

During the 1920s, Germany (which was known as the Weimar Republic at that time) experienced a period of hyperinflation. The price of bread doubled in the span of a few days and the German people had to use banknotes worth millions or even billions of marks (the currency used at the time).

SUMMARY

- Money does not have a constant value; its worth fluctuates over time.
- Inflation is a mechanism which limits households' purchasing power through an overall price increase. It is measured using a representative consumer basket of goods and services which reflects consumer spending habits.
- Deflation is the opposite of inflation, and can be defined as a general price drop. This situation halts economic growth, because economic agents will delay making purchases. This is because they know that prices will continue to fall and they want to get the best deal possible.
- Inflation is caused by factors such as excess demand for products and services, increased production costs or excess money supply.
- Businesses are less likely to invest during periods of inflation, because it creates a climate of economic uncertainty.
- Inflation decreases returns for lenders and

is beneficial for borrowers, as the real value of the sums that they have to pay back will decrease over time.

- During periods of inflation, it is best to invest in shares and raw materials; conversely, it is better to buy fixed-rate bonds and open fixed-term savings accounts during periods of deflation.
- When you are planning to make an investment, you should take inflation into account in order to work out the present value of the eventual dividends.
- Central banks consider inflation to be preferable to deflation. This is why the European Central Bank maintains a rate of inflation which is close to, but does not exceed, 2%.

We want to hear from you!
Leave a comment on your online library
and share your favourite books on social media!

FURTHER READING

BIBLIOGRAPHY

- Akerlof, G. A., Dickens, W. T. and Perry, G. L. (1996) The Macroeconomics of Low Inflation. *Brookings Papers on Economic Activity.* [Online]. [Accessed 9 November 2017]. Available from: <https://www.brookings.edu/bpea-articles/the-macroeconomics-of-low-inflation>

- Blanchard, O., Amighini, A. and Giavazzi, F. (2017) Macroeconomics: A European Perspective. 3rd edition. Edinburgh: Pearson Education Limited.

- Brealey, R., Myers, S. and Allen, F. (2016) *Principles of Corporate Finance.* 12th edition. New York: McGraw-Hill Education.

- Chartoire, R. and Loiseau, S. (2014) *L'économie. Retenir l'essentiel.* Paris: Nathan.

- Daniel, J. (2014) *Manuel d'économie.* Paris: Ellipses.

- European Central Bank. (No date) *What is inflation?* [Online]. [Accessed 9 November 2017]. Available from: <https://www.ecb.europa.eu/ecb/educational/hicp/html/index.en.html>

- Eurostat. (2017) HICP all items. *Europa.eu.* [Online]. [Accessed 9 November 2017]. Available from: <http://ec.europa.eu/eurostat/web/

- products-datasets/-/teicp000>

- Fisher, I. (1922) The Purchasing Power of Money. The Macmillan Co. 2th edition. [Online]. [Accessed 9 November 2017]. Available from: <http://www.econlib.org/library/YPDBooks/Fisher/fshPPM8.html>

- Lecaillon, J., Le Page, J. and Ottavj, C. (2008) *Économie contemporaine, Analyses et diagnostics.* 3rd edition. Brussels: De Boeck.

- Leroux, E. (2011) Comment doper son épargne en profitant de l'inflation. *LaTribune.fr.* [Online]. [Accessed 9 November 2017]. Available from: <http://www.latribune.fr/vos-finances/epargne/20110408trib000614210/comment-doper-son-epargne-en-profitant-de-l-inflation.html>

- Mankiw, N. G. (2014) *Brief Principles of Macroeconomics.* 7th edition. Boston: Cengage Learning.

- Shafir, E., Diamond, P. and Tversky, A. (1997) Money Illusion. *The Quarterly Journal of Economics.* 112(2), pp. 341-374.

- Sloman, J., Wride, A. and Garratt, D. (2012) *Economics.* 8th edition. Edinburgh: Pearson Education Limited.

ADDITIONAL SOURCES

- Eurostat. (2017) Inflation in the euro area. *Europa.eu.* [Online]. [Accessed 9 November 2017]. Available from: <http://ec.europa.eu/eurostat/statistics-explained/index.php/Inflation_in_the_euro_area>

- Inflation.eu website: <http://www.inflation.eu>

Although the editor makes every effort to verify the accuracy of the information published, 50Minutes. com accepts no responsibility for the content of this book.

www.50minutes.com

Ebook EAN: 9782808000352

Paperback EAN: 9782808000369

Legal Deposit: D/2017/12603/445

Cover: © Primento

Digital conception by Primento, the digital partner of publishers.